Holiday Recipe Box

The Thanksgiving Cookbook

Mary Lou Caswell and Deanna Caswell

BLACK RABBIT BOOKS

Hi Jinx is published by Black Rabbit Books
P.O. Box 3263, Mankato, Minnesota, 56002.
www.blackrabbitbooks.com
Copyright © 2021 Black Rabbit Books

Marysa Storm, editor; Michael Sellner, designer;
Omay Ayres, photo researcher

Names: Caswell, Mary Lou, author. | Caswell, Deanna, author.
Title: The Thanksgiving cookbook / by Mary Lou Caswell and
Deanna Caswell.
Description: Mankato, Minnesota : Black Rabbit Books, [2021] |
Series: Hi jinx. Holiday recipe box | Includes bibliographical references. |
Audience: Ages 8-12 | Audience: Grades 4-6 | Summary: "Teaches readers
how to make simple and delicious Thanksgiving treats through clear
directions and illustrated steps"– Provided by publisher.
Identifiers: LCCN 2019026719 (print) | LCCN 2019026720 (ebook) |
ISBN 9781623103125 (hardcover) | ISBN 9781644664087 (paperback) |
ISBN 9781623104061 (ebook)
Subjects: LCSH: Thanksgiving cooking–Juvenile literature. |
Cooking–Juvenile literature. | Food craft–Juvenile literature. |
LCGFT: Cookbooks.
Classification: LCC TX739.2.T45 C37 2021 (print) |
LCC TX739.2.T45 (ebook) | DDC 641.5/68–dc23
LC record available at https://lccn.loc.gov/2019026719
LC ebook record available at https://lccn.loc.gov/2019026720

Printed in the United States. 1/20

Image Credits

Black Rabbit Books: Cover, 6, 7, 8, 9, 10, 11, 12, 14–15, 18, 19; iStock: from_my_
point_of_view, 8; HitToon, 7, 9, 10, 12, 15; nata_vkusidey, 9; Rebekkah_ann, 6;
Tigatelu, 2–3; Shutterstock: Arcady, 5; A-Star, Cover;
AVS-Images, 20; borsvelka, Cover; drawkman, 1,
21, 23; GraphicsRF, 4–5; HitToon, 4; Jozsef
Bagota, 17; larryrains, 1; Memo Angeles,
Cover, 10–11, 13, 14–15; Monstar
Studio, 20; opicobello, 12–13;
Pasko Maksim, 17, 23, 24;
pitju, 7, 15, 21; Ron Dale, 5,
6, 9, 17, 20; totallypic, 7,
17, 18; tablespoon.com:
Hungry Happenings, 18;
Every effort has been made to
contact copyright holders for material
reproduced in this book. Any omissions will be
rectified in subsequent printings if notice is given to the publisher.

CONTENTS

Chapter 1

Thankful for Thanksgiving

Thanksgiving is a time for family. People think about what they're thankful for. They watch parades and football games. They eat LOTS of food too. Get into the Thanksgiving spirit with dishes of your own.

Don't forget to have a trusty adult by your side. Have them help with any cutting or tricky steps. They can also watch out for foods your guests might be allergic to.

Supplies

knife

cutting board

medium
mixing bowl

large spoon

plastic wrap

Ingredients

½ cup
(120 milliliters)
pecans

12 ounces
(340 grams)
whipped cream
cheese

6 ounces (170 g)
dried cranberries

8-ounce (230-g)
can pineapple
tidbits, undrained

Chapter 2

The
Recipes

Cranberry Dip

Cranberries can be sour. No one will make sour faces at this dish, though. It's a super **savory**-sweet treat!

1. Chop the pecans into small pieces.

2. Put the pecans in a bowl with the rest of the ingredients.

3. Mix the ingredients together with the spoon.

4. Cover the bowl with plastic wrap.

5. Refrigerate the dip overnight. Give it a good stir before enjoying with crackers.

This dip will serve eight people.

Corn Cakes

American Indians taught Pilgrims how to grow corn. Have corn at your holiday celebration.

Supplies

large mixing bowl
mixing spoon
medium mixing bowl
whisk
frying pan, coated with cooking spray
¼ measuring cup
spatula

Ingredients

15-ounce (420-g) can unsalted corn, drained

2 eggs, lightly beaten

½ cup (120 ml) 2% milk

2 tablespoons (30 g) butter, melted

8 ounces (230 g) shredded cheddar cheese

½ cup (60 g) flour

½ cup (80 g) yellow cornmeal

2 tablespoons (30 ml) dried **chives**

1 teaspoon (5 ml) salt

¼ teaspoon (1.25 ml) pepper

Serve your corn cakes with honey or butter.

This recipe makes about 14 corn cakes.

Steps

1. In a large bowl, stir together the corn, eggs, milk, butter, and cheese.

2. In a medium bowl, use the whisk to combine the remaining ingredients.

3. Add the flour mixture to the corn mixture. Use the spoon to stir them together.

4. Heat the pan over medium heat.

5. Drop ¼ cup (60 ml) of batter onto the pan. Flatten the batter slightly with the back of the measuring cup.

6. Cook the cake for two to three minutes on each side. Use the spatula to turn the cake.

7. Repeat Steps 5 and 6 until you've used all the batter.

Turkey Salad Bunwiches

They don't call it Turkey Day for nothing. There is so … much … turkey! Turn leftovers into yummy bunwiches. Everyone will gobble them up.

This recipe feeds four people.

Supplies

medium mixing bowl

mixing spoon

¼ measuring cup

tinfoil

baking sheet

pot holders

Ingredients

6 ounces (170 g) shredded Swiss cheese

1 cup (240 ml) chopped cooked turkey

½ cup (75 g) diced celery

1 teaspoon (5 ml) onion powder

½ teaspoon (2.5 ml) salt

⅛ teaspoon (.6 ml) pepper

¼ cup (60 ml) mayonnaise

8 hamburger buns

Steps

1. Preheat the oven to 400 degrees Fahrenheit (204 degrees Celsius).

2. In a bowl, stir together all of the ingredients except the buns.

3. Spoon about ¼ cup (60 ml) of the mix onto a bottom bun. Press on the top.

4. Wrap the bun in tinfoil. Place it on the baking sheet.

5. Repeat Steps 3 and 4 until you've used each bun.

6. Bake the buns for 10 minutes. Use pot holders to remove. Unwrap and enjoy!

Gobble Taco Pizza

Turkey, tacos, and pizza … together?
It sounds crazy, but it's delicious!

This pizza feeds six people.

Supplies

pizza pan

rubber spatula

medium
microwafe-safe bowl

mixing spoon

pot holders

Ingredients

12-inch (30-centimeter)
prebaked pizza crust

9 ounces (250 g) bean dip

1 cup (240 ml) shredded
cooked turkey

1 cup (240 ml) salsa

1½ cups (350 ml)
shredded Mexican cheese

1 cup (240 ml)
corn chips, crushed

1. Preheat the oven according to the crust package's directions.

2. Place the crust on the pan.

3. Using the spatula, spread the dip on the crust.

4. Place the turkey and salsa in the bowl. Stir them together with the spoon.

5. Microwave the turkey and salsa on high for one minute. Stir.

6. Spread the turkey mix on top of the dip.

7. Sprinkle the pizza with cheese.

8. Sprinkle the corn chips on top of the cheese.

9. Bake as the crust package directs. Remove from the oven using pot holders.

Chocolate Turkey Cake

Are you sick of turkey? Don't turn up your beak just yet! This turkey is so sweet. You'll be happy to have one more slice.

This dessert feeds eight people.

Supplies

2 9-inch (23-cm) cake pans, sprayed with cooking spray

pot holders

serving plate

butter knife

4 small bowls

knife

cutting board

6 6-inch- (15-cm-) long wooden skewers

Ingredients

1 15.25-ounce (432-g) box chocolate cake mix

16-ounce (450-g) container chocolate frosting

2.25-ounce (63.8-g) jars red, yellow, and orange colored sugar

17 large marshmallows

2 chocolate chips

Turn the page for steps.

Steps

1. Preheat the oven to 350 degrees Fahrenheit (177 degrees C).

2. Prepare the cake mix according to the directions on the package.

3. Divide the cake batter evenly between the two pans.

4. Bake the cakes for 30 minutes. Remove them from the oven with pot holders. Let them cool completely.

Tip Frosting a cake is harder than it looks! Don't be afraid to ask your adult for help.

5. Once the cakes have cooled, remove them from the pans.

6. Place one cake on the plate. Use a knife to frost its top with about 2 tablespoons (30 ml) of frosting.

7. Place the second cake on top of the first. Use all of the frosting to cover the top and sides. It doesn't need to be smooth.

8. Dump each color of sugar into its own bowl. Fill another bowl with water.

9. Cut one marshmallow in half diagonally. One piece will become the bird's beak. The other will become the **snood**.

Turn the page.

10. Skewer one marshmallow half. Dip it in the water. Then roll it in yellow sugar. Remove the marshmallow from the skewer. Set it aside.

11. Repeat Step 10 with the other marshmallow half using red sugar. Set it aside.

12. Skewer, dip, and roll 15 whole marshmallows. Roll five in each color of sugar.

13. Thread one marshmallow of each color onto a skewer. Poke the skewer into one edge of the cake.

14. Repeat Step 13 with four more skewers. Your bird now has feathers!

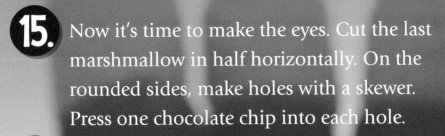

15. Now it's time to make the eyes. Cut the last marshmallow in half horizontally. On the rounded sides, make holes with a skewer. Press one chocolate chip into each hole.

16. Place the eyes on the cake's top. They should be opposite the feathers. Put the beak beneath the eyes. Put the snood to the side of the beak.

Chapter 3

Get in on the HiJinx

There are many careers that involve working with food. One of them is food stylist. These artists make food beautiful before photographers take pictures. Some foods don't photograph well. Food stylists use special tricks to make them look better. Motor **oil** stands in for pancake syrup. They use soap bubbles for **frothy** foods. Maybe one day you'll be a food stylist!

Take It One Step More

1. Benjamin Franklin wanted a turkey to be the U.S. national bird. Research to find out why.

2. Taco pizza is a **fusion** dish. Fusion foods combine several countries' **cuisines**. What are some fusion foods you can think of?

3. Imagine you're a food stylist. Which recipe in this book would you style? Would you need any tricks to make it photograph better?

GLOSSARY

allergic (uh-LUR-jik)—having a medical condition that causes someone to become sick after eating, touching, or breathing something that is harmless to most people

chive (CHAHYV)—a plant that is related to the onion

cuisine (kwi-ZEEN)—a style of cooking

frothy (FRAW-thee)—full of or made up of small bubbles

fusion (FYOO-zhuhn)—a combination or mixture of things

oil (OYL)—a greasy liquid substance

savory (SEY-vuh-ree)—having a spicy or salty quality without being too sweet

snood (SNOOD)—the fleshy part at the base of a turkey's bill

tidbit (TID-bit)—a small piece of food

BOOKS

Heinecke, Liz. *Kitchen Science Lab for Kids: 52 Mouth-Watering Recipes and the Everyday Science that Makes Them Taste Amazing.* Beverly, MA: Quarry Books, 2019.

Kids Bake! 100+ Sweet and Savory Recipes. New York: Hearst Books, 2018.

Varozza, Georgia. *The Sugar Smart Cookbook for Kids.* Eugene, OR: Harvest House Publishers, 2019.

WEBSITES

Holidays for Kids: Thanksgiving Day
www.ducksters.com/holidays/thanksgiving_day.php

Kid-Friendly Thanksgiving Recipes
www.highlights.com/parents/recipes/15-kid-friendly-thanksgiving-recipes

Recipes & Cooking for Kids
kidshealth.org/en/kids/recipes/

TIPS AND TRICKS

Mind the rules of the kitchen. Wash your hands. Be careful with hot food and sharp tools.

Always clean up after yourself. Cooking for others is great. It's not great if you leave them with chores.

If guests can't eat nuts, don't add them to the cranberry dip. For a crunch, add unsalted sunflower seeds instead.

The bunwich recipe works well with other meats and cheeses too. Try chicken and cheddar.